The Seeds You Sow Stage Play

Written & Soon to be Produced
By: Luther T. Collins

The Seeds You Sow
Stage Play

Written & Soon to be Produced
By: Luther T. Collins

Printed in the United States of America by
Ingram Spark
www.ingramspark.com

© Copyright 2020 by Luther T. Collins

All rights reserved. This book or parts thereof may not be reproduced in any form, stored in a retrieval system, or transmitted in any form by any means-electronic, mechanical, photocopy, recording, or otherwise-without prior written permission of the author, except as provided by United States of America copyright law.

All Music, All Poetry, All Spoken Word Written & Created by Luther T. Collins.

ISBN: 978-1-7351253-0-5

To contact author for booking or ordering additional copies, go to:
luthertcollins0408@gmail.com

Message to the World

My thoughts and prayers are with everyone world-wide during this trying time we are experiencing in today's society. During times of crisis we come together and fight as one. Together we stand and divided we fall. Tough times don't last always and what can't kill you can only make you stronger.

Covid 19 also known as the Corona Virus is deadly, destructive, and devastating. However with that being said the God I serve is greater than any name, including Corona or Covid 19. God has the final say so and I'm a true believer that the best is still yet to come.

Since we can't physically go to theatre I wanted to take the time to bring the theatre to you. This is nontraditional and unheard of but I believe this will bless you, encourage you, and inspire you. God gave me PMP – Productions Made Personal as this is only the beginning. We are in a season of creative content where the creative's are coming to the forefront.

Intro

This play was written in 2008 as I'm happy to say this was the first of many plays that I would write. I have not performed or produced this play but it is my pride and joy as I wanted to share it with the world. It's always good to laugh when you're experiencing trying times. I believe that "The Seeds You Sow" will not only bless you but it will give you insight and inspiration from different perspectives.

In 2008 I was a manager at KFC and a young lady by the name of Jennifer Mason came through drive thru. She had a promotional label on the side of her SUV of an upcoming production that she had written. The name of the play was called Chaos in the House. After speaking with her and telling her I was an aspiring writer she gave me two free tickets to the show. After seeing the show I was so inspired that I wrote my first play. Prior to meeting her I was only writing books and had not even tapped into or experienced playwrighting.

Without further or due I give you, "The Seeds You Sow" stage play in a book.

Table of Contents

Scene 1   Daddy's Home

Scene 2   Change of Heart

Scene 3   I'm in Charge

Scene 4   Junior Returns Home

Scene 5   She's Gone

Scene 6   Final Goodbye

Scene 7   First Official Sermon

Scene 8   Reminiscing Moments & Memories

Scene 1 – Daddy's Home

Terry: Hey baby I'm home I just got my paycheck (Flashing money)
Bernanese: Boy you so crazy you know you don't work no where
Terry: Take that back I put in hours just like you
Bernanese: What's your supervisor name? Hugh?
Bernanese: Where's your pay stubs? Hugh?
Bernanese: And how come you didn't file taxes the last 10 years?
Terry: I don't have to answer to you woman? Where my boys at?
Bernanese: Upstairs where else you think they gone be?
Bernanese: Boys your daddy's home
Boys: (Running down stairs pushing each other out the way)
Junior: What's up pops? What about those Giants?
Terry: We might be losers but you know I got to roll with my Cowboys
Junior: Even though they washed up
Terry: They not washed up they just a little under the weather

Junior: That's right dad keep hope alive, just keep telling yourself and one day you'll believe that, sike
Westley: (Pushes Junior out the way) Move out the way punk, I want to speak to dad too
Junior: (Mushes Westley in the face)
Terry: Junior you better leave your brother alone
Junior: Yes Dad
Westley: Hey dad I missed you, where you been?
Terry: Well son I been working overtime all day today, how else I'm going to pay for them Jordan's?
Westley: We got career day coming up at school will you be able to come and talk about your job?
Bernanese: (Laughing out of control)
Terry: You find something funny
Bernanese: Yea I called your job today and they said you were on an extended vacation
Terry: You pushing it woman
Terry: Yea I'll come son if I'm not at work
Westley: By the way dad what's the name of your job and what kind of work you do
Bernanese: Terry why don't you ask Tommy from Martin

Terry: Bernanese I told you, you pushing it woman. I'm a business man for a universal corporation son
Westley: Okay dad
Bernanese: That ain't what the boy asked you and how come I never heard of this company before
Terry: Bernanese
Bernanese: Yes my ever so hardworking husband what can I do for you? Are you hungry my dear I know you're tired form working all of that overtime?
Terry: Shut up woman
Westley: Dad I wasn't finish, can you help me with my science project
Terry: Sure son
Trevon: Dad don't forget about me
Terry: What's up my little buddy I haven't forgotten about you
Terry: Your mama just getting on my nerves right now
Bernanese: Do they get on your nerves like that at work to?
Bernanese: Naw let me leave you alone boy before you pass out from all that hard work today
Trevon: Dad I need you to put my transformer man back together again

Terry: You brokem again, you know them transformers not cheap you know
Trevon: Dad I tried to break up the fight but Spider Man and Batman jumped Optimus Prime
Terry: Whatever you just betta keep them action figures out of intensive care, I'm not going to keep paying their hospital bills
Trevon: But dad I need my action figure men
Terry: You heard what I said boy
Terry: Come on Westley let's go knock out this project
(Knock on the door)
Junior: Who it is
Dope Dealer: Yo Daddy now open the door punk
Junior: Yo mama now tell me who you are (Opens up the door in curiosity)
Dope Dealer: Shut up boy and go get your dad
Bernanese: (Mom stands up looking furious)
Junior: Who you talking to?
Bernanese: I don't know who you think you're talking to like that but you in the wrong household for that

Dope Dealer: (Flashes gun and says) Now go get your daddy (Grabs him by the collar and pushes him forward) before I lose my patience, boy
Bernanese: (Yells in concern) Terry get your but downstairs now
Terry: (Comes down stairs) Who is it?
Dope Dealer: (Points gun at Terry) Mr. Dillion says to give you this (Shoots him 8 times)
Bernanese: (Hollering and screaming as the gun fires)
Boys: (Holler for their dad as the gun fires) Lights Dim

End of Scene 1

Scene 2 – Change of Heart

Pastor Jordan: Dear beloved Smith family we are gathered here today to celebrate the life of Mr. Terry Lucinnelly Jovalenne Sampsonite Smith. He was a handsome looking man and that's all we know about him. He said he had a job but I never knew where he worked. Though he never made it to the house of God I think he had intentions. One thing I do know about Mr. Terry Smith is he loved his children and wife dearly. I'm sure his death came as a surprise to us all so I encourage everyone today don't leave out of the house without being saved. And for those of you who are saved repent and turn from you wicked ways. Stop lying to your spouse about where you been
Sister Susie Mae: Amen, Pastor (Stands up waving her wrinkled handkerchief)
Pastor Jordan: Stop your cheating on the down low having minajatwas with the same sex
Sister Susie Mae: Amen Pastor (Stands up waving her wrinkled handkerchief)
Pastor Jordan: Stop stealing knock off wigs from the dollar tree

Sister Susie Mae: Amen Pastor (Stands up straightening up her knock off wig)
Pastor Jordan: Stop putting expired food stamp dollar bills in the offering plate and for the last time you cannot pay your tithes with food a stamp card although we will accept charitable donations for the hospitality ministry
Sister Susie Mae: Amen Pastor (Stands up waving her food stamp card)
Pastor Jordan: Stop using your children's names for your light bills and telephone bills
Sister Susie Mae: Amen Pastor (Stands up waving her wrinkled handkerchief)
Pastor Jordan: Got an apartment in your son or daughter name I never heard of such foolishness in all my days
Sister Susie Mae: Me neither Pastor (Sitting down waving her hand)
Pastor Jordan: And please stop using me as a reference when you apply for welfare
Sister Susie Mae: (Stands up with her wrinkled handkerchief but Pastor spoke before she could get the words out)
Pastor Jordan: I ain't gone say no names though, Sister Susie Mae.
Sister Susie Mae: Naw Pastor that was my sister Shaquita I told her to stop it but she won't listen Pastor

Pastor Jordan: Sister Susie Mae
Sister Susie Mae: (Jumps up out of her seat with urgency in joy) Yes Pastor
Pastor Jordan: You know a woman can go to hell for lying like she can for stealing
Sister Susie Mae: (Sits down and shuts up)
Pastor Jordan: Now before we close let's hear from the family members
Bernanese: He was my first, my last, my everything
Sister Susie Mae: (Interrupts) Hey girl, ain't that Barry White
Bernanese: Shut up Susie, like I was saying before being interrupted Terry wasn't that much of a believer but he was a good husband and father with a good heart and I'll miss him dearly (Sniffling, begins to cry)
Junior: (Comes and escorts his mom to her seat and goes up to podium) I love my dad and just don't understand why anyone would want to take his life. I will miss him a lot (Takes his seat)
Westley: (Walks up to the podium with Trevon holding his hand) We love you dad and miss you (They began to walk back to their seats)
Pastor Jordan: Before we bring this home-going service to a close I just want to say there may be someone here today that does

not know the Lord, Jesus Christ as their personal savior. Mr. Smith's brief stay just goes to show tomorrows not promised and if you were to die tomorrow and your name's not written in the lamb's book of life you can't make it into the kingdom. You don't wait until you get yourself together because nobody's perfect you come as you are and let God work out your problems. Anyone who wants to receive Jesus Christ as their Lord and Savior on today please come on down to the altar. Remember tomorrows not promised and hell is hot. Mr. Smith was 35 years old and won't even be able to see his children grow up nor his children's children. Don't wait for tomorrow because tomorrow may never come.

Bernanese: (Walks down to the altar crying)

Pastor Jordan: Is there anyone else (Pauses), okay stretch your hands towards her and repeat after me. Father you are the Christ, Son of the living God, I believe you died for me set me free, forgive me of all my sins, right now I change my ways and make Jesus Lord and Savior of my life therefore I am saved. Come into my heart Jesus.

Pastor Jordan: (Hugs Bernanese and pulls her to the side) Are you okay?

Bernanese: Yes Pastor I'm okay I just can't believe he's gone maybe God's trying to get my attention
Pastor Jordan: You know we're here for you if you need us
Bernanese: Yes I know Pastor
Pastor Jordan: Hey Bernanese would you be interested in filling our church clergy position, it's very demanding, and requires some long hours at times but we will pay you $3.00 an hour
Bernanese: Yes sir when do I start and where do I sign up
Pastor Jordan: Come on into my office and we'll get the paperwork started now
Bernanese: (Fills out paperwork and works her first shift as the church clergy answering telephones, setting up appointments, aiding the pastor, and helping with the order of the church)

Lights Dim: Bernanese walks to center of stage and begins to sing!

Hold on

(Chorus)

If I just hold on
Hold on Lord
If I just hold on
Hold on father
If I just hold on
(Pause)   You'll save me

Verse 1

From the clouds that form
To the storms that pass
For the troubles they seem
So steadfast
But you told me Lord
If I hold your hand
And divorce the world
You'd change my plans
As tomorrow's unknown
But your glory is shown
So much fullness in you
Lord ----- what do I do

(Chorus)

Verse 2

Peaceful days will come
From the house of healing
Lord restore my mind
Give me a new feeling
As I connect myself
To your vision in life
Seeking to serve the king
I'm a living sacrifice
Please anoint my soul
Insert me with wisdom
As I live for you
And follow your vision

(Chorus)

Verse 3

Lead me to the anointing
The circle of life
Where the kingdom has come
Give me eternal life
Make me whole again
Wash me in your blood complete
You're my only true friend
For I know not defeat

(Chorus)

End of Scene 2

Scene 3 – I'm in Charge

Junior: Yall know since moms not home that means I'm in charge now I need yall to go upstairs because I got company coming over
Westley: What you going to be doing that we can't stay downstairs
Trevon: Yea Junior why we can't stay downstairs with you
Junior: Because I said so now go upstairs
Westley: Man I'm telling mom when she gets home
Trevon: Me to
Junior: Whatever just get the stepping (Trevon and Westley walking upstairs angry) (Knock at the door)
Westley: Trevon go in the room and close the door and I'll be in there in a minute I need to speak with Junior (Goes back to the steps to peep around the corner to see what's going on)
Trevon: Okay but don't forget about me
Junior: Who is it?
J Smooth: Its J Smooth man now open up the door
Junior: What's up Smooth you got my heat?
J Smooth: Yea you got my green

Junior: Yea (Making exchange drugs for gun)
J Smooth: Where your peoples at?
Junior: Moms working at the church, you know she been working like a slave since pops passed she won't be in until tomorrow morning and my brothers upstairs
J Smooth: You know I got the scoop on the suckers that killed your pops
Junior: I hear they hang out at Ocean View on Hillside Dr at them apartments behind the 7 Eleven
J Smooth: Yea but Mr. Dillion is where everyone gets there product from, your dad owed him some money and your father told him he wasn't paying him because he was robbed so Mr. Dillion ordered a hit out for him. He paid Murder 2 g's to kill your pops
Junior: I'm going to take his life just like he did my pops after I re up
J Smooth: We'll let me know if you need anything homeboy
Junior: Aight I'll holla at you later
(J Smooth leaves the house)
Westley: Goes in room with Trevon (Calls mom and says mom please come home ASAP we really need you it's urgent)
Junior: (Yells for Westley) I'll be back West watch Trevon I got to run an errand

Westley: Be careful
Junior: I'm just running out real quick I'll be back if mom call tell her I went next door
(Junior leaves house)
(Westley and Trevon comes down stairs)
Trevon: Where's Junior
Westley: He had to run out for a minute
(Bernanese walks in as she rushes home from work)
Bernanese: Hey boys, West I got home as soon as I could, what's wrong what's so urgent that you called me at work
Westley: Trevon go upstairs I need to speak to mom in private please
Trevon: But I didn't even get to speak to mom
Bernanese: Come here baby give me a hug, how's my big boy
Trevon: I miss you mom, since dad left you're always at work and I never get to see you
Bernanese: I know baby, run upstairs for me and after I speak with your brother we'll play with your action figures, how does that sound
Trevon: Good mom
(Trevon runs upstairs)

Westley: Mom, Junior got a gun and I think he's selling drugs with those same guys that always used to stop by and see dad
Bernanese: Are you sure? How do you know this baby?
Westley: That J Smooth guy came over and I heard him tell Junior that Mr. Dillion paid some guy name murder to kill dad
Bernanese: Okay baby thank you I'll handle it from here. I need you to do me a favor and go watch your brother please. Do not let him out of your sight. I already lost your dad and I refuse to lose any of you.
(Westley goes upstairs)
(Bernanese prays for Junior)
(Junior comes walking in the house)
Junior: Mom what you doing home I thought you were suppose to be at work
Bernanese: The question is where have you been you were supposed to be watching your brothers and what's this foolishness I hear about you having a gun?
Junior: It's just for protection mom
Bernanese: Come here boy, (Looking at Junior) where did you get that necklace from? I know you're not dumb enough to be out there selling drugs too

28

Junior: Well somebody has to do something I'm tired of eating oodles and noodles every night. I mean look at us we had to sell the TV to pay the light bill. And I haven't had a new pair of Jordan's since dad died

Bernanese: Son I know a lot has changed since your father has died but I'm not going to see you die just like your father did. There will be no drugs and no guns in this house. Do I make myself clear?

Junior: Mom I respect what you're doing and all but I can't live like this and I'm going to take care of Mr. Dillion myself (Junior walking out)

Bernanese: Don't be stupid Junior (Bernanese breaks down in tears)

End of Scene 3

Scene 4 – Junior Returns Home

(Trevon walking downstairs)
Trevon: Good morning mom
Bernanese: Good morning baby you hungry
Trevon: Yes mam, hey mom
Bernanese: Yes baby
Trevon: When is Junior coming home I miss him
Bernanese: Soon baby
(Westley walking downstairs)
Westley: Morning mom
Bernanese: Good morning baby
Westley: What's for breakfast
Bernanese: Your favorite eggs, bacon, and grits now come on to the table so we can say the grace
Westley: I'll say the grace mom
Bernanese: Okay go ahead
(Everybody holding hands at table)
Westley: Father I pray that you bring Junior home safely and that he won't die amen
Bernanese: That's good baby but what about the food
Westley: Good food good meat thank God let's eat
Bernanese: Survey says errant try again
Westley: Thank you Lord for this food we

are about to receive please bless it and bless the cook amen
(Everybody eating)
(Junior comes walking in the door)
(Everybody stops eating and runs to give him a hug)
Bernanese: I take it you came to your senses boy; don't you know the seeds you sow are the seeds you grow? You owe this family an apology, you got me and your brothers worried about you
Junior: I'm sorry yall I missed being at home
Bernanese: Now come sit down and eat so I can talk to all of you
Junior: Yes mam
Bernanese: Your daddy was a drug dealer and that life just caught up with him. Promise me that you boys will stick together and finish school and go to college.
Boys: (Altogether) We Promise Mom
Bernanese: Junior that would require you returning back to school
Junior: I know mama

Bernanese: We are all we got and we must stick together. Don't ever let anyone tell you what you can or can't be. I want you boys to go out and make me proud of you. If you don't know anything else I want you to know that I love you.
Westley: Mom how come you always at the church all the time
Bernanese: Because I work there and I made a promise to God when your father died that I would serve him until I died and in return God promised he would save my boys
Junior: That will be the day especially when God let my daddy die
Bernanese: God did not let your daddy die you can't expect God to save you if your living for the devil. You better learn to be grateful for what you do have. He woke you up this morning in your right mind, you have food to eat, and he didn't even charge you for the air you breathe
Junior: I guess so mom but I'm just not ready to change yet I still have some more living to do
Bernanese: Son you never know when it's your time to go as your father didn't and nothing on earth is worth burning in hell for remember that

Trevon: I love you mom
Bernanese: I love you to baby
(Knock at the door)
Bernanese: Westley go get the door
Westley: Who is it
J Smooth: A friend of the family
(Westley opens the door)
(J Smooth walks in with Mr. Dillion)
J Smooth: Oh junior I forgot to tell you Mr. Dillion is my brother
Mr. Dillion: What's up blood I hear you were looking for me, I don't normally make house calls but I wanted to save you a trip
Bernanese: Boys go upstairs now
J Smooth: (Flashes his gun) Naw I think everyone needs to stay down stairs
Bernanese: Now I don't know what's going on but you two need to leave my house now
Mr. Dillion: Yes mam right after me and Junior exchange some words
Junior: I don't have nothing to say to you, you had my dad killed man (Flashes his gun)
J Smooth: (J Smooth points his gun straight at Junior's head) Nobody move nobody gets hurt
(Bernanese steps in front of Junior)

Mr. Dillion: Fine have it your way
(Pulls out his gun and shoots Bernanese 6 times)
(Westley grabs Trevon and they duck under the table)
(Junior just stands behind Bernanese in shock as she falls back on him)
Mr. Dillion: Our job is done let's get out of here
(Mr. Dillion and J Smooth leaves)
(Boys crowds around there mom)
(Trevon crying)
(Westley crying)
(Junior calls ambulance)
(Bernanese hanging on for dear life trying to get some words out)
Bernanese: (Gasping for air) Junior take care of your brothers (Passes out)

End of Scene 4

Scene 5 – She's Gone

Westley: (All hysterical calls Pastor Jordan and asks him if he can come down to the hospital to be with him and his brothers)
Boys: (Sitting in the lobby waiting for the doctor to give them an update)
Junior: (Pacing back and forth in the hospital)
Trevon: (Crying aloud I want my mommy)
Dr. Long: Hey boys your mom is in critical condition were actually surprised she made it this far, we don't know how long your mother will live as your more than welcome to go in and see her but we ask that you be extremely quiet and go in 1 at a time
Westley: Dr. Long, can I go in with my little brother because he can't go alone
Dr. Long: That's fine son
Bernanese: God please take care of my boys and save them (Praying while clinging on to dear life)
Trevon and Westley: (Going in room to see their mother together)
Westley: Hey mom you okay, the doctor says you may not make it but I know you'll be okay
Trevon: Yea mom you're going to be okay right?

Bernanese: I don't know boys I'm in a lot of pain and I feel weak. Promise me something before you leave out of here
Westley: Anything mom
Bernanese: Promise me you will take care of each other and pray to God for strength if I don't make it
Westley: I promise mom
Trevon: I promise too
Dr. Long: Alright boy's times up we still got one more visit
Trevon and Westley: We love you mom (Hugs mom tightly before leaving)
Bernanese: I love you too now go and make mama proud
Dr. Long: Come on you got 5 minutes young man your mom needs to rest
Junior: Yes sir (Walks into room with mom)
Junior: Mom I am so sorry I didn't know
Bernanese: (Interrupts) Stop baby just promise me you're going to get your life together and make something of yourself. Promise me if I don't make it you will take care of your brothers. Promise me you won't sell drugs and carry guns. Promise me you will seek God first before making decisions and his way of doing things when you get into a bind.

Junior: I promise ma but why did you take those bullets for me I'M SUPPOSE TO BE IN THE HOSPITAL LAID UP, NOT YOU
Bernanese: I have lived my life baby now it's your turn besides God wants to use you to spread the gospel of his kingdom
Junior: What do you mean mom
Bernanese: (Turns away from him, takes her last breath, and dies)
Junior: Mom, Mom, Say something
(In shock he realizes mom just died)
Junior: God I don't know if you can hear me but please take good care of my mom
(Junior leans over to kiss his mom on the cheek)
Junior: Good bye mom, I love you mom
(Junior walks out of the room back into the waiting room with brothers)
Junior: She's gone
Westley: Nooooooooo, Nooooooooo, Not mama
Trevon: (Begins to cry loudly)
Pastor Jordan: (Arrives at hospital and greets the boys as he tries to comfort Trevon)
Westley: It's all your fault Junior if you wouldn't never got caught up with J Smooth and them she would still be here
Junior: Shut up Westley (The boys go back

and forth as Trevon cries louder and louder)
Hospital Security: (Security comes over and threatens to kick the boys out)
Pastor Jordan: (Separates Westley and Junior until they calm down) I know it's not easy boys as this will be the hardest thing you will ever face but you must be strong and pray for God to give you strength. One thing about your mom she was a very strong woman and always prayed that God would keep you boys together. Now is the time for you boys to come together. Nothing you can do will ever bring her back. I will help you as much as I can but I need you guys to help me prepare for her funeral. Let us pray. (Instructs the boys to hold hands as he prays for them in the hospital)
Pastor Jordan: Amen
(The boys all sit down in the hospital as Pastor Jordan walks to the center stage to sing a song)

Although I'm down and out
And I don't know what to do
I'll lift my hands and praise
Lord I worship you

So many times before
I felt so out of place
Running from the world
As the tears leave my face

Can you listen to my story
Hear me loud and clear
Let him that have an ear
Receive this message without fear

I lost my mom and dad
Thought it was all I had
Until you came to me father
And said don't look so sad

He said I am your way my child
For I'm the light and the truth
And if you follow me right now
I'll restore your youth

Just Open your heart and receive
Expand your mind to believe
No need to worry or fear
I'm Jehovah and I'm right here

Drop your burdens
And leave them behind
Walk on the word in the storm
And I'll restore your mind

For I'm the prince of peace
Nobody's greater than me
Come on home come get your keys
Divorce the world and follow me

I love you
You are my child
Rejoice with me
And I'll make you smile

And in end when I return
You'll go with me
I'll keep you safe in my arms
As I restore your family

So the next time you're down and out
And you don't know what to do
Hold me in your heart oh so close
And I'll do the rest

End of Scene 5

Scene 6 – Final Goodbye

Pastor Jordan: Praise the Lord everyone
Audience: (A couple people respond) Praise the Lord
Pastor Jordan: (Raises Voice) I SAY PRAISE THE LORD EVERYONE
Audience: (Everyone responds, loudly in unison) Praise The Lord
Pastor Jordan: For the Lord is good and his mercy endures forever! Today I want to take the time and reflect on our very own Sister Bernanese Smith. For this is the day that the Lord has made so we will rejoice and be glad in it. We are not going to mourn because we know she wouldn't have that. Sister Bernanese Smith was a strong, beautiful, and highly anointed child of God. She was so full of wisdom, love, and always willing to give her last to anyone who asked. Today she leaves behind 3 awesome young men to carry on her legacy. Junior Smith, Westley Smith, and little Trevon Smith. I can only imagine how much it hurts to lose such an incredible mom. But one thing I want you to understand today is that God makes no mistakes. We all must go on one day and only God knows when our time is up. I know the transition will not be easy

but we as your church family here at Dominion Visions Powerhouse of God want to let you know that we are here for you and we love you with the love of the Lord. I also want to let you know that there is no failure in God. Remember children mom is now in the pretty blue skies above and she sees everything you do. Before I give the boys an opportunity to speak Westley has written a poem he would like to share. Come on up young man
Westley: (Walking up all slowly)
Pastor Jordan: Come on up young man we all family don't be shy (Goes and helps him up to the podium)
Westley: (Recites poem)

I wonder why as I look up at the sky
My tears form but they just won't cry
It's like I hear your voice calling my name
Similar to before but just not the same
Sensing a little more calm and a little more peace
Something like a massive celebration with a mighty feast
Yet I can't comprehend what I don't understand
Losing my mom but it was all a part of the master's plan

As my flesh is still trying to accept what's already done
Trying to rationalize telling myself the war has already been won
But questioning if I'm on the winning team
As I can no longer convince myself this is just a dream
For I just realized that materials can't make a man
Losing my most valuable treasure on earth made me to understand
Tired of looking ahead at what tomorrow will bring
Mom you said to praise the Lord so I will continue to sing
I sing because I'm happy I sing because you're forever free
Even though you can't hold me your still inside of me
And before I leave earth to join you in the kingdom above
I promise I'll make you proud beginning with sharing your love!

Audience: (Everyone stands while clapping as his brothers give him a hug as he returns to his seat)

Pastor Jordan: That was beautiful Westley

your mom is smiling down on you. Junior come on up and share some words on behalf of your mom
Junior: I just want to apologize to my brothers for my choices as my mom would still be here I just (Breaks down while speaking)
Westley: (Walks up and hugs him tight) It's alright bro (Escorts him back to his seat)
Trevon: (Walks up to the podium) I love you mom and we all miss you. You take care and be good okay! I promise to do my best in school and keep up with my action figures since there's no one left to pay their hospital bills (Trevon goes to sit down).
Pastor Jordan: We'll yall now that we said our goodbyes. I want you all to join in this song I wrote. I'll do the singing and you just sing the chorus (Pastor begins to sing).

Lift your hands and praise him with me

Father you are my soul
I submit to your control
We worship you for who you are
More than a conqueror that's who you are
It's on today that we confess
In your arms where we rest
No more lonely days to see

As we surrender unto thee

So lift your hands and praise him with me

Our father who art in heaven
You hear my voice you hear my cry
You comfort me like a sweet lullaby
Thank you for your mercy
Your endless glory
Abide in me set me free
I was a sinner
For you rescued me

Everybody sing with me

Father you are my soul
I submit to your control
We worship you for who you are
More than a conqueror that's who you are
It's on today that we confess
In your arms where we rest
No more lonely days to see
As we surrender unto thee

So lift your hands and praise him with me

Victorious in your will
Communion time
Let's seal the deal

*I'll follow you all by myself
Not concerned with no one else
Jehovah Jireh
You are my provider
I want for no good thing
For my desires you will bring*

Everybody sing with me

*Father you are my soul
I submit to your control
We worship you for who you are
More than a conqueror that's who you are
It's on today that we confess
In your arms where we rest
No more lonely days to see
As we surrender unto thee*

So lift your hands and praise him with me

*I worry not, cause I have you
There's no limit on what you can do
My bible says it in your word
Speaking what I know not what I heard
I love you more with each passing day
You took my burdens and washed them away
For gratefulness cannot describe
The abundant joy I have inside*
Everybody sing it with me

*Father you are my soul
I submit to your control
We worship you for who you are
More than a conqueror that's who you are
It's on today that we confess
In your arms where we rest
No more lonely days to see
As we surrender unto thee*

So lift your hands and praise him with me

Pastor Jordan: (Benediction while chorus being sung in background) If there's anyone who doesn't know the lord at this time press your way to the altar. For tomorrow's not promised and that's the only way you can see the king. You don't have to be perfect but come as you are and God will do the rest.
Boys: (All come down to the altar with deep expressions of tears and sadness)
Audience: (Everyone stands up clapping)
Pastor Jordan: Will there be anyone else? Somebody's heart is beating fast. This may be your last chance.

Sister Susie Mae: (Crying loud, comes running to the altar and loses her old wrinkled handkerchief and knock off wig while on her way to the altar)

Pastor Jordan: Now church everyone stretch your hands towards them and repeat after me: Father you are the Christ son of the living God I believe you died for me set me free forgive me of my sins I've done wrong but right now I make Jesus lord and savior of my life. Come into my heart Lord as it's on today that I confess that I am saved use me for your kingdom in a mighty way. Amen (Pastor congratulates boys and Sister Susie Mae and then congregation comes down to do the same in the form of hugs and handshakes)

End of Scene 6

Scene 7 – First Official Sermon

Pastor Jordan: It's good to be in the house of the Lord one more time if I may say so myself, Junior wanted me to let everyone know he was running a little behind but he would be here
Sister Susie Mae: Amen, Pastor
Pastor Jordan: Today we are celebrating in the graduation and going away of Brother Westley Smith. He graduated high school today and will be heading off to college in the fall. Congratulations on your success young man as we speak limitless blessings and favor upon you in your journey. We know your mom is so proud of you. Brother Wesley graduated from Norview High School class of 2008 with honors and has a full scholarship to Harvard where he plans to become a doctor. Since the departure of their mom 3 years ago Wesley, Junior, and Trevon have all took on rolls in the church and contributed to our growth success. I wish you all Gods Speed in everything you do. And Westley as your church family we have a couple of surprises for you. First we have a gift just for your faithfulness, obedience, and success as a young man. We are so proud of you and love you dearly.

Wesley: (Walks up to get the gift and turns to go back to his seat)
Pastor Jordan: Westley, now you know we are not going to let you off that easy (Hands Westley the mic just before he could make it back to his seat)
Westley: I just want to say thank you to my church family and Pastor, Pastor Jordan. I really appreciate all the love and support over the years as I could not have done it without you. Thank you to my brothers Junior and Trevon who helped me deal with the toughest situation that we ever had to face. I love you all and will keep you all in my prayers. Be blessed.
Audience: (Everyone stand and claps)
Westley: (Returns to seat and sits down)
Pastor Jordan: God bless you young man. And just when you thought we were finished we have not even begun to get started. Westley we have a special treat for you today. Your brother is watching us on TV; he's in my office preparing for his first official sermon
Westley: (Stands up) SERMON
Pastor Jordan: Yes you heard that correct he's been really on fire for God since your mother passed. He took over her role as church clergy, enrolled in bible school, and

asked me not to tell anyone. He wanted it to be a surprise. God was preparing him as this young man is ready to preach the gospel to the world. Without further delay I give you Minister Junior Smith
Trevon: (Stands up) Mom I hope you're watching
Junior: (Walks in prepared to bring the word of God to the saints)
Minister Smith: Praise the Lord saints
Congregation: Praise the Lord Minister (Altogether in unison)
Minister Smith: Today we gone talk about Walking in the fullness of the blessing as this is the year of extravagance. Turn with me if you will in your bibles to Psalms 37:11. When you get there say Amen!
Congregation: Amen
Minister Smith: Let's all read together
Congregation: (Everyone reading dysfunctional and not together)
Minister Smith: Stop! I said together
Congregation: (Everyone reads together) The humble shall inherit the land and enjoy prosperity
Minister Smith: Now let's think about this the humble shall inherit the land. Another word for humble is meek. Ask yourself can you put others before yourself? Another

word is obedient; did you do the last thing God told you to do? Another word is loyal, were you loyal when your Pastor said pay your tithes? Another word is faithful, were you faithful to your spouse? Another definition is true to your word, can I trust you or do I have to watch my back? When we talking about humble were talking about someone whose kingdom minded and puts God before his own wants and needs. Did you pray before you got up and ate breakfast? Did you consult with God before consulting with the world? Do you talk to God or do you just use him as a foot stool? Only pull him out when you need something? It's mighty quiet in this Presbyterian Church. I'm talking to somebody up in here. Being humble is being a servant without complaining and worrying. And for your humbleness your reward shall be great. It says you will inherit the land does anybody have any land? I said is there anybody who wants to be some land owners? Somebody might show up and give you a farm. Or show up and give you a business office all because you were humble. And if you have some land God said he's getting ready to give you some more land. Anybody ready for some increase on today? Do you want some houses? Some property? Some businesses? Well keep on being humble and watch God show up. And for your humbleness you'll enjoy abundant prosperity all your days. Prosperity is peace, joy, happiness, the ability to do what you couldn't do before, kingdom living. And in abundance, to the fullest, till your cup runneth over. Oh I'm talking up in here. I don't know about yall but I want some of this land and abundant prosperity. Some of yall say well preacher how do I get it. By being humble. Let go of those situations that got you bound and give them to God. Divorce the world and turn from your wicked ways. God said he will never put you to shame. God said he will open up the windows of heaven and flood you with so many blessings you won't be able to receive them. Just be faithful and he will do the rest. If you sin don't wait repent right then for your land may be held up in sin. Don't wait on the world just stay in God by working the word and he'll do the rest. Amen.

Benediction

That concludes my word for today if there's

anyone who doesn't know the lord today is your day. If there's anyone who seeks some of this land and abundant prosperity today is your day.

(3 people go up)

Minister Smith: Hallelujah! Praise the Lord for you have just made the biggest decision of your lives and God is going to bless you. Now everyone stretch your hands towards them and repeat after me. Father you are the Christ, son of the living God, I believe you died for me, set me free, forgive me of my sins, I've done wrong but right now I make a decision to change my ways. I die to the world so I can live for Christ. I make Jesus Christ Lord and savior of my life therefore I am saved.
Minister Smith: (Hugs them and shakes their hands)
Congregation: (Comes up to congratulate them in the form of hugs and handshakes)
Trevon: Hey yall I got a surprise to, I got a song that I just wrote while I was in my seat and I may need some help so feel free to join in. I dedicate this to my mama Bernanese Smith it's called Oh So Proud
Westley: We'll let it rip

Audience: (Everyone stands up and starts clapping)

Trevon: *She would be oh so proud*
Congregation: *Where is she now*
Trevon: *She would be oh so proud*
Congregation: *Where is she now*

Trevon: *My mama used to say*
Congregation: *Hallelujah*
Trevon: *God is the way*
Congregation: *Hallelujah*
Trevon: *And when my time is up*
Congregation: *Hallelujah*
Trevon: *God will fill your cup*
Congregation: *Hallelujah*
Trevon: *He'll never leave you alone*
Congregation: *Hallelujah*
Trevon: *So put down that telephone*
Congregation: *Hallelujah:*
Trevon: *Turn from your evil*
Congregation: *Hallelujah*
Trevon: *He'll turn you into a believer*
Congregation: *Hallelujah*
Trevon: *And that's all I have to say*
Congregation: *Hallelujah*
Trevon: *Cause God is the way*
Congregation: *Hallelujah*
Trevon: *But before I say goodbye*

Congregation: Hallelujah
Trevon: No you won't see me cry
Congregation: Hallelujah
Trevon: Mama we love you so
Congregation: Hallelujah
Trevon: But mama we got to go
Congregation: Hallelujah
Trevon: Thank you for your prayers
Congregation: Hallelujah
Trevon: That brought us oh so far
Congregation: Hallelujah
Trevon: You turned us into fishermen
Congregation: Hallelujah
Trevon: Mom, we know not no sin
Congregation: Hallelujah

Trevon: *She would be oh so proud*
Congregation: *Where is she now*
Trevon: *She would be oh so proud*
Congregation: *Where is she now*

Trevon: *Up in the kingdom so high she can touch the sky*
Congregation: *Hallelujah*

End of Scene 7

Scene 8 – Reminiscing Moments & Memories

Trevon: What's up Minister Smith Aka Big Bra I knew I could find you here
Minister Smith: What's up man? Dang boy you grow up so fast. I remember it seems like just yesterday when you were that little boy chasing me around crying about some action figures now you riding around in your 760IL BMW and just graduated high school going to play pro ball. Who would have ever thought?
Trevon: Me
Minister Smith: Boy you so crazy
Trevon: And by the way I still got my action figures but they like souvenirs now
Minister Smith: Yea you just keep telling yourself that
Trevon: Man who would have ever thought that after mom passed we would have made it this far
Minister Smith: Surely not me, And I want to apologize for setting the bad example for all those years

Trevon: That's okay because I know God was preparing you for something much greater than any of us could ever imagine. I'm so proud of you and I know mom is to. Besides what else was you going to do, it ain't like you can play ball or something
Minister Smith: Oh you got jokes right, we'll at least I don't like them washed up Cowboys
Trevon: We'll just because your Giants won the super bowl doesn't mean they all that
Minister Smith: You just missed two key words super bowl which means champions and giants which mean ain't nobody better. Don't be a hater all your life. I remember I had to give dad the same life lessons from the football perspective
Westley: (Walking up)
Trevon: What's up doc? All you need now is a carrot and you'll be bugs bunny
Westley: Ahh you got jokes? Well all you need now is some color and you'll be black
Minister Smith: Yall crazy what's up man
Westley: I knew I could find yall here just getting in town you know I couldn't miss moms birthday, so what's up, we gone sing or what yall

Minister Smith: Can't nobody sang like old Minister Smith
Westley: All right Eddy Cain
Trevon: You want my spot flash well you can't get it cause you ain't got it
Westley: Aight Ike and Mike come on let's sing Happy Birthday to mom
Boys: (Sing happy birthday to their mom)
Happy Birthday to you Happy birthday to you Happy Birthday dear mom Happy birthday to you
How old are you How old are you How old are you How old are you May God bless you May God bless you May God bless you May God bless you
Remix
Happy Birthday to ya, Happy Birthday to ya Happy Birthday
Minister Smith: *And we do mean you*
Trevon and Wesley: (Laughing in joy)
Minister Smith: So what's up doc, congrats on that doctrines degree. I hear you started your own hospital
Westley: Yes Sir, Actually God started it, I just applied for the position and got the job it just so happened it was my own business
Minister Smith: What you think of Mr. Action Figure Man himself going straight to the NBA from high school

Trevon: Yo Mama

Westley: Yall know she heard that, right

Minister Smith: Trevon mom said to tell you stop playing with those doll babies in the spiritual realm

Trevon: Well mom told me to tell you that you can't play basketball with a broken jump shot. She said to tell you don't pass go don't collect $200 but go to the shop immediately and get a tune up

Westley: Yall boys crazy. Trevon you a bad Mammy Sammy going into the NBA in the first round and since Big Bra over there ain't told you yet I'm a let you know God is really moving

Trevon: What you talking bout Willis?

Westley: Minister Smith is getting his own church built from the ground up; it's all ready over half way done

Trevon: Say What

Minister Smith: Well I was going to surprise yall when it was done. How you find out

Westley: Well you know Pastor Jordan can't hold water

Minister Smith: Yea you right about that

Westley: Man I can't keep up with yall boys but I tell you what that song you started at church for mom really inspired me and you know it got boring in college sometimes so what I did is started working on a gospel hip hop album and it's actually set to be released in 30 days. Yall wanna get a lil taste
Minister Smith: Can you smell what the Roc is cooking?
Trevon: Yea I can smell it but I don't know if I'm a like it. I used to listen to rap even after I got saved but when Jay C out right disrespected God with that CD Lucifer I kind of lost interest in rap all together. Just because they ready to die and anxious to go to hell doesn't mean I'm in agreement. So Westley I'll hear but I don't know if I'm listening
Westley: This ain't no Apollo and you ain't Sandman so sit yo little booty down and listen besides this is for mom any way

When I got lost
I found myself looking for you
My heart was searching for you
You turned my grey skies blue
It's only you, it's only you, it's only you

Thrown into this here game
Left with heartache and pain
I was sowing nothing but rain
I made you so ashame
Mama won't you forgive me
I was caught in my ways
Lost a lot sleep
Skipped over many days
And then I came into the light
Distinguished darkness from night
I gave my worries to Christ
He restored my sight
And now I'm turning to you
Oh how I miss you

When I got lost
I found myself looking for you
My heart was searching for you
You turned my grey skies blue
It's only you, it's only you, it's only you

Mama we love you so
We'll never let you go
For you made us who we are
Living legends by far
No more generational curses
Tired of riding in these hearses
So we gave our problems to the lord
As he supplies all our needs

So we thank you mama so much
For doing more than enough
To get us up in the sky
Until we meet again up high
This is our goodbye

When I got lost
I found myself looking for you
My heart was searching for you
You turned my grey skies blue
It's only you, it's only you, it's only you

Boys: (All drop a rose and say goodbye at their mom's grave and all walk out together)

End of Scene 8

This Concludes The Play

Written by Luther T. Collins 9/30/2008

Upcoming Arrivals

The Seeds You Sow Tee Shirts will be available in the near future for purchase. There is no current definitive date for the production of this play. For information regarding this or future productions please contact luthertcollins0408@gmail.com.

Thank you for supporting my God Given – God Inspired vision!

Productions Made Personal Volume 1 will be released in the summer of 2020!

"The Seeds You Sow"

Sow a seed
And watch it grow
And in due time
Your harvest will overflow

© September 2008
Written by Norfolk Native
Luther T. Collins

The Seeds You Sow
Stage Play

Written & Soon to be Produced
By: Luther T. Collins